Copyright © 2024 by Pippa Bird

All rights reserved. No part of this book may be reproduced or transmitted in any form or by any means, electronic or mechanical, including photocopying, recording, or by any information storage and retrieval system, without permission in writing from the publisher.

ISBN: 9781763733961

First Edition

Posy's Special Find

Pippa Bird

In a serene riverbank in the Australian wilderness, there lived a cheerful platypus named Penelope.

This particular platypus was known for her sunny outlook on life and her ability to find the silver lining in any situation.

One morning, Penelope was swimming along the river when she noticed her friend, Posy the Possum, looking glum.

Posy sighed, "I have lost my favorite pink shell in the river. Now I feel so sad because I cannot swim or dive to find it."

Penelope thought for a moment and then said, "Oh, but I can. Let me have a look for you."

Posy waited patiently while Penelope disappeared beneath the water.

Penelope dived into the river in search of her bush friend's favourite shell.

She searched the riverbank beneath the water.

She searched behind the river rocks and weeds on the riverbed.

She even searched the deeper parts of the riverbed where the water was darker.

But Penelope soon returned to the riverbank with no such luck.

She climbed out of the water and slowly shook her head. "I'm sorry, Posy. I could not find it anywhere," said Penelope.

Posy curled herself up into a ball, her tail hugging her body as she sulked. She was very sad.

"I understand how losing something special can be upsetting. But maybe this is a chance to find a new shell that's even more amazing!"

With Penelope's encouragement, Posy's spirits lifted just a little.

"Let's go on a shell hunt together," suggested the platypus. Posy sat up, intrigued.

The bush friends spent the rest of the day searching the riverbank.

Together they found wonderful, new, exciting things.

Slow, slimy, sluggy things.

Things that come from the river...treasure.

One piece of treasure the possum admired the most.
A white river pebble.

Posy thought it extra special because it was the shape of a heart.

"Oh, Penelope, I love it even more than my lost one because we found it together."

"Hooray!" said Penelope, throwing her arms into the air.

"Whenever I look at it, I will be reminded of you and our special friendship," gushed the possum.

The bush friends continued their day searching for treasures along the riverbank. Posy was grateful to have such a helpful, happy friend like Penelope.

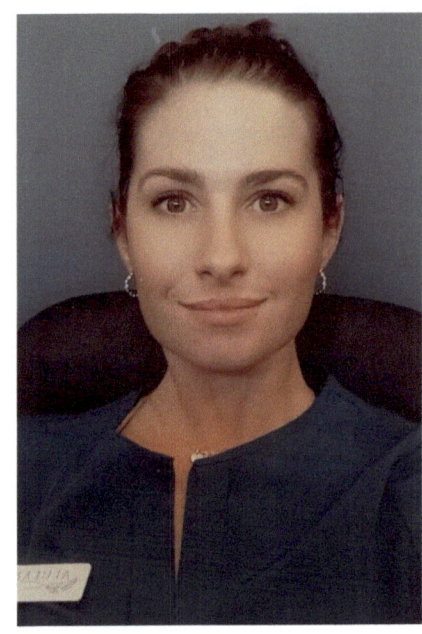

Calm Kangaroo

About the Author

Pippa Bird is a Mental Health Therapist in Private Practice in regional NSW. Pippa holds a Bachelor in Psychology, a Diploma in Counselling, and is currently undertaking a Postgraduate Degree in the field.

Pippa also holds a Diploma in Graphic Design, with a primary focus on illustration.

CALM KANGAROO is a backronym title for a children's mental well-being program. An initiative designed to educate children about mental health and foster a learning journey of emotional intelligence, resilience and cultivate an open mind through the power of reading well-being books, leading to the most important discussions and ideas.

The CALM KANGAROO program focuses on **C**urating, **A**dvocating and **L**eading **M**indfulness and its mission to **K**indle **A**wareness, **N**urture **G**rowth, **A**mplify **R**esilience, and **O**rchestrate **O**pen-minds.

Calm Kangaroo is an Alula Blu Initiative

www.ingramcontent.com/pod-product-compliance
Lightning Source LLC
Chambersburg PA
CBHW041544040426
42446CB00003B/225